INDICE

Monaco Woman is dedicated to the woman, but not only. An open window on a world where beauty, fashion, and lifestyle blend in harmony with glamour, elegance and history that have always distinguished the women world. We will involve our readers in the world of beauty participating them in the most important events and accompanying them to discover the most exclusive places in the world. We promote the image of the real woman, the woman who knows how to fascinate, not only for her beauty, but also for her beauty, but also for her spirit and her abilities. Mum, Model or Manager, our women will always be the mirror of reality.

Editor & Founder
Alessia Castelli.

The structure of today's society is complex and twisted, but this does not limit women's determination to shine. Women are constantly tested in whatever role they play, to overcome these ideological barriers there is need of determination, strength, and coalition. We want to create a "refuge" where you can relax but at the same time feel inspired by the stories of resourceful women, with the determination to stand out, create concepts, products and services that look at uniqueness, sustainability, and respect for the environment.

MONACO
———
WOMAN

La vita
mi ha resa
fragile e forte
allo stesso
tempo.

CRAZY PIZZA
MONTE CARLO

CIPRIANI
MONTE CARLO

GOURMET

BB
BY BONTAR
Côtes de Provence
BB
BY BONTAR
Côtes de Provence

A HIDDEN TREASURE IN THE HEART OF CENTRAL VAR: THE DOMAINE DE LA CROIX DE BONTAR

Nestled amidst the hills and vineyards in the beautiful region of Central Var, there is a vineyard steeped in history and passion. Originally, this land was the farm adjacent to a castle, bearing witness to a rich past. Its name, «Domaine de La Croix de Bontar,» evokes the goodness of this fertile land that has endured through the ages. The Segond Family Winery, preserving a family tradition of over 30 years, is a wine treasure that embodies the soul of Provence.

With its 35 hectares of vineyards, the Domaine de La Croix de Bontar captures the richness and diversity of the region's terroirs. This year marks an important milestone in the domain's history, with the completion of the third harvest, followed by the very first limited bottling, which was met with great success. The Domaine has committed to transitioning to organic farming, prioritizing environmentally friendly methods. Vinification takes place entirely on-site in a new cellar, ensuring absolute control over the quality of the wine throughout the production process. Significant investment in the restoration of the vineyards has brought picturesque dry-stone walls back to life and reinstated a historic network of wells for natural irrigation. The result is a preserved and authentic terroir.

The wines By Bontar are already present in several renowned restaurants in the Principality of Monaco and the surrounding areas, including Norma, Chez Pierre, the African Queen, and new establishments are continually joining this expanding list.

A Word from the Producer

It is with immense pleasure that we announce our first blend of Côte de Provence rosé wine, an authentic expression of our sun-soaked terroir and our passion for the art of winemaking.

This rosé, delicate and fresh, embodies the very essence of Provence. Its light color recalls the sunsets that bathe our vineyards, while its floral and fruity bouquet evokes the Mediterranean scents that perfume our estate. We are eager to share this treasure with you, to invite you to savor this enchanting rosé with your loved ones and let it reveal its secrets as you share glasses. But this is just the beginning of our wine adventure. Our estate is brimming with promises and other treasures to discover.

Exceptional vintages, deep reds, elegant whites, and much more await you in the heart of our vineyards.

Tasting

With its peach-colored robe and silvery highlights, the initial aroma is intense, featuring notes of citrus, blackcurrant buds, and exotic fruits like passion fruit. After swirling, hints of white peach emerge. The palate has a generous first impression. The mid-palate is supported by the flavors of exotic fruits. The finish is fresh and exhibits a lovely salinity.

Aldea Segond

MONTENAPOLEONE
1817

TWIGA
MONTECARLO

W VILLADORATA
COUNTRY RESTAURANT
WITH VIVIANA VARESE

Foto: ©Mattia Aquila

The respect for the raw material, sustainability, the enhancement of a territory and its biodiversity, are the principles of the kitchen of Viviana Varese in Noto. The star chef and entrepreneur Viviana Varese, for the third consecutive year has returned to Sicily, in Noto, where she reopened her project W Villadorata at the Country House Villadorata. A return to its origins for the Chef, for whom it has always been important (re)connect with the sun, nature, the earth. We know her for her VIVA, a Michelin star, inside Eataly Smeraldo in Milan, and for her strong social commitment to women. Among the hills of Val di Noto, halfway between the city with its churches, noble palaces, and the countryside, lies Country House Villadorata, within an estate that extends over 25 hectares, surrounded by olive groves, almond trees, citrus groves and a small vineyard. The attention to the land starts from the use of the recovery of pruning of citrus, olive trees, almond trees as firewood for the fire and for the new kitchen of the restaurant, both inside, with the new room overlooking the surrounding countryside, and outside. So much so that from 2022 Country House joins the Alliance Slow Food, a pact between cooks and small producers to promote good food, right and clean of the territory, and to save biodiversity. The Alliance's chefs use every day in their

kitchens the products of farmers, breeders, cheesemakers, fishermen, winemakers, artisans who produce with passion and respect for the land and their animals. All the fruits of the trees of Villadorata become juices, extracts and candied fruit to offer at breakfast, in the rooms and in the shop of VIVA. All the crops of the estate of Villadorata follow the biodynamic method, which does not involve the use of pesticides and fertilizers, and considers the land as an organism to be protected and of which to optimize its fertility. Safeguarding the planet in all its forms and limitation intensive exploitation of crops, livestock, seas are our priority. For Viviana Varese and Country House sustainability is not a concept linked only to the use of the raw material, but also to the choice to collaborate both with small artisans, protecting and enhancing their work, both with social cooperatives including Si può fare of Noto and Eta Beta of Bologna. The principles of this unique experience are the enhancement of the territory and its biodiversity, respect for raw materials and ingredients used in dishes, all accompanied by the joy of the restaurant.

In the menu of the restaurant, local products are the protagonists, in addition to vegetables, tomatoes and aromatic herbs, also flour of ancient grains such as thymine and majorca, oil, citrus; unique dishes prepared through smoking, fire and oven, characteristic of the kitchen of Viviana Varese and that tell its roots. The wines on the menu are mainly of Sicilian origin, there are bubbles, biodynamic, ancestral wines and Marsala D.O.C at the end of a meal. There are also craft beers and a menu of cocktails whose scents recall the land of Sicily. The land is VIVA (alive), that is why Viviana Varese chose Country House Villadorata, a place that perfectly reflects the gastronomic ethics of her cuisine. A magical place to "get your hands dirty" and cultivate the passion of doing, as the chef explains: "Nature chooses and decides, follow its mood and its power, with respect, joy and gratitude, is one of my primary values". From 2022 to carry out the project are two former sous chef of VIVA, both with an experience of several years alongside Viviana Varese who have also collaborated with the Chef for the new openings of Io sono VIVA desserts and ice creams in Milan: Matteo Carnaghi, now Executive Chef of W Villadorata and Ida Brenna, Pastry Chef together with a young team both in the kitchen and in the dining room trained at VIVA in Milan. The local productions, the ingredients, the Slow Food Presidi of the island inspire them in the creation of new recipes, along with some historical dishes by Viviana Varese.

An indoor room has a wood-burning kitchen, a total experience with seats at the counter to watch the show. A la carte menu where the flavors of the raw materials of Val di Noto and Sicily are enhanced by the creativity of the

> A magical place to "get your hands dirty" and cultivate the passion of doing

Chef. The choice between the tasting paths includes: a menu of the four elements, a gastronomic journey of nine courses through the sea and the land, in the island of the sun and its flavors to discover the elements in which nature takes shape (surprise of the Chef), an air menu and a water-land menu with two dips in the sea and two steps in the garden.

All obviously with the possibility of matching the wine pairing with three, five or eight glasses, or non-alcoholic matching with 4 glasses. A place to live, to taste and to discover, with a chef who has created a team and a project that "are worth the trip"!

Nadia Toppino

BB
BY BONTAR

FASHION

GENNY

GENNY
THE ORCHID GARDEN

Milan, September 21st, 2023

Shades of white. Infinite, reasoned, imperceptible, more visible. An exercise in style that embraces the entire new GENNY collection, Spring-Summer 2024. Sara Cavazza Facchini, creative director of GENNY, repositions the focus on the interpretation of luminosity in relation to the female body. White has always been her quintessential color. Her aesthetic practice finds a comfort zone in the dialogue with the optical neutrality of natural glow. In fact, the iconic choice of a total white horizon is the choice that Sara Cavazza Facchini has made since the dawn of her creative experience with GENNY. It is an important path that has now come to celebrate its first 10-year anniversary.

The new GENNY collection is the representation of lightness, the most candid and soothing one. Sara Cavazza Facchini's work focused on the materialization of an aura that accompanies the everyday life of a constantly brilliant woman. In this artistic context, the care in revealing the body assumes a pivotal role. It is not revealed, but emerges.

It delicately emerges from the clothes, confronts light and its shading, through the hyper-selective and qualitative choice of fabrics. Silks, chiffons, georgettes, crumpled cottons, carded linens, are the tailoring fabrics that participate in the construction of the seductive fluidity of the collection that faces GENNY's Spring Summer 2024.

Sara Cavazza Facchini's styling work ensures the silhouette of physicality the most natural expressive freedom. Body volumes are present, but never tight. They are slippery, soft, accepting lines. The collection unveils in a habitat with a strong tropical feel: an orchid garden, a symbol of GENNY's sensuality. The dresses, the suits, the whole collection is punctuated and emphasized by two ancestral elements. On the one hand, the presence of precious metals: yellow gold, rose gold and platinum. Inserts that make the wardrobe more material. On the other, the presence of the iconic orchid that becomes an embroidery, a brooch, a second identity signature. The synthesis of this vocation is in a must have piece of the collection: the orchid-chiseled metallic bodice. That identifies the transition from the ethaereal to the concrete, giving a propulsive boost to GENNY's glamorous vocation. Accessories are consequential to the expression of primal naturalness. A web of weaves identifies belts, bags, footwear. Inevitable is the seasonal variant of the Block Chain, the material expression of knitted fabric designed by Sara Cavazza Facchini is a regular fixture. Almost a capsule in the collection that generates anticipation in GENNY's target community, populated with celebrities like Jennifer Lopez. For Spring-Summer 2024, consistent with the sense of cozy luxury conveyed throughout the collection, the Block Chain is embroidered with crystals and miniaturized with metal laminations.

Tania Beker

In the heart of Milan fashion week, city that embodies timeless elegance and design, the fashion world will witness an explosion of creativity and innovation with the GX Fashion Week. This exceptional event will break expectations as every year, to give the public an experience that will capture the attention and heart of all, precisely for the refined celebration of diversity and eclecticism, nothing but justice to the universal language. Once again some of the most daring and visionary minds in the glamorous world from all over the planet will be gathered, creating an enchanting mosaic of cultures, styles and trends that will leave the audience speechless. In this edition the focus will be on the celebration of fashion as a global art form and as a vehicle to express individual eccentricity, taste and refinement, in the context of creativity and stylistic diversity that will stand out in the foreground. During the past editions, the GX Fashion Week saw an extraordinary variety of cultural influences converge on the catwalk. From the bright colors of Latin America to the minimalist lines of Northern Europe while, on 23 September 2023, at 15, at the Corridoio Leonardo of the Fondazione

WEEK

Stelline in Milan, Corso Magenta 61, will be the explosion of ideas and inspirations to ensure uniqueness and considerable level of choices in which believed Gentiana Dervishi, President of the Association APS Showteam whom, assisted by a team of considerable experience, will guarantee, as in every other occasion passed, a consistent afternoon tied to the fashion, whose yardstick of choice and preliminary evaluation have proved extremely careful and selective without distinction between emerging or established designers. «Subject to previous editions, reason for my personal joy, given the media feedback bounced on several magazines dedicated around the world, I think that September 23 not only reflects the same feedback, but that exceeds the expectation of anyone. Organizing a fashion show, with many designers, of certain sizes, requires a lot of effort that involves not only me, but a staff prepared and numerous, composed of reliable people who care about winning outcomes, exactly as myself. Only the ancient concept of team, meticulously applied, allows successes. Clothes on the catwalk worn by models, Make-up Artist team, together with the staff deployed behind the scenes, will be the perfect mix to interpret excellent tailoring styles, with the aesthetic mood created by APS Showteam», these are the statements of Gentiana Dervishi, an eclectic artistic mind with very clear ideas, compared to the technical dynamics that will be linked during the day of the fashion shows. Many designers who will show off on catwalks wonderful Creations, including Umberto Perrera (Sartoria Perrera), Elsida Pepa (ada – Albanian Design Academy), Khalil Malek (Séléné Haute Couture), Sonila Harizi ed Aleks Harizi (DSA - Dream Store Albania), Fouad Guerfi (Fouad Couture), Owana Lima (Nicteel), Claudia Cinzia Atella (Claude Couture Creation), Francisco Rodrìguez

(Chacabanas Faraòn), Cristian Fortunato (Hola Mosa - Men's Collection), Margarita Kola (MK - Atelier Margot). «One of the distinctive features of this edition will be the audacity to export the unexplored territories of fashion. Beyond the sartorial wisdom I intend to clear up what has never been lived on the catwalks. Designers will dare bold combinations of colors, unusual fabrics and dresses that will challenge the normally desirable conventions. Experimentation will be the focus of attention, with every designer trying to overcome the limits of creativity» concludes the "Patron" of the event, finally pressing on the «Awareness referred to the environmental issues, where the GX Fashion Week Milano will put the attention to take a step forward in the promotion of sustainability. Many designers will present creations made with refined materials, as well as thematic, eco-friendly techniques and responsible approaches. This commitment to sustainability will show that

THE CATWALKS WILL HIGHLIGHT THE WONDERFUL MULTICULTURAL UNIVERSE OF FASHION

fashion can be at the forefront by limiting the damage to our beautiful planet» underlines APS President Showteam. It is important to emphasize how valuable will be the artistic and professional contribution of makeup artists and hairdressers who, through unique experience regarding the ornamental contest of models, will apply with flair and professional touch the mood created by the Organization of the event. Coordinators of the Hair Stylists Corrado Costanzo, which will be assisted by Armanda Cerbella, while the Make-up Artists will be directed by Daniela Zeqo. GX Fashion Week has attracted the attention of celebrities and iconic fashion influencers from around the world. Each piece that will alternate will outline a unique work of art, ready to capture the imagination of the public, while to welcome will be the wonderful environments of the Fondazione Stelline, located in the heart of Leonardo's places, just where once they had found fertile soil the roots of the vineyard of the great Renaissance artist, the "Orti di Leonardo", in front of the Cathedral of Santa Maria delle Grazie where is preserved the most famous mural painting in the world, the Last Supper.

Sara Rockman

METAMORPHOSIS AND THE PASSION OF LOVE WITH ELISABETTA DELOGU

"Inspiration pushes me to tell forms transformed into new bodies."
Thus sings Ovid – (Métamorphoses, I. 1-2)

The stylist Elisabetta Delogu is divided between her showroom in Milan and her workshop in Sardinia for many years and she represents an inimitable reference in the universe of the wedding. She develops wedding dresses, evening dresses, exceptional and refined. Its unique collections, a selection of timeless pieces, both classic and offbeat, are sublimated by precision work and the choice of precious materials.

Nothing seems to stop the stylist who puts forward all her unique know-how, her dazzling imprint and allows all the audacity. Elisabetta Delogu leads us to a new potential of seduction that questions us on the impression of extreme beauty of each creature. The transformation of a body between unity and diversity.

This is the power of creativity: knowing how to highlight each individual with its own language and beauty.

What is the theme of this new collection entitled Metamorphosis?

Metamorphosis is the change, mutation, transformation of a being or an object into another of a different nature, but also the change, the modification of the appearance, character, attitude of a person. Elisabetta Delogu's season of Metamorphosis opens with a couture capable of representing form and appearance with astonishment and wonder, at the whim of the imagination. Creativity asserts itself as the tool capable of promoting a metamorphosis that is not only internal. Metamorphosis is a collection

marked by severe features, veiled with frivolous sacrality, adorned with erotic fragments, spiritual passion. It is the surreal tale of a season of metamorphosis and transformation. Ode to freedom and the spirit of transformation!

Karine Patricola

FREEDOM

TRANSFORMATION

CHAMBRE MONEGASQUE
DE LA MODE

MONTE-CARLO FASHION WEEK

JEWELS

DOUBLE/FACE TANGIBLE AND INTANGIBLE IN ART JEWELRY

Exhibition at Miart, Milan

Club degli Orafi Italia, an independent Association representing the most important Italian goldsmiths companies, participated in MIART, the international fair of modern and contemporary art in Milan, with an exhibition featuring the concept of the double or of the interior/exterior related to jewelry and art. The exhibition was curated by Alba Cappellieri, Full Professor of Jewelry and Fashion Accessories at the Polytechnic University of Milan where she is also director of the international Master in Fashion Accessories Design.

This fascinating theme is well interpreted by the eight jewelry artists and brands: Alfredo Correnti, Angeletti 1940, Cesari & Rinaldi Gemmai, de' Nobili, Liverino 1894, Mattioli, UNOAERRE and Vhernier.

What for some might seem a narrative device, Double Face in jewelry is a real moment of revelation and a cause for reflection about the inner duplicity of jewelry, both for the preciousness of materials and manufacturing and for the creativity, innovation and avant-garde spirit. The unifying element of this double-sided aspect is the art which makes us think about the meaning of "precious" in the contemporary world.

Giorgio Villa, President of Club degli Orafi Italia, declared: "I am proud to present Club degli Orafi's first participation at Miart. There is such a strong link between art and high-end Italian jewelry. Over the centuries the incredible skills of Italian goldsmiths have, on many occasions, joined forces with the creative flair of internationally known artists, whose maestria in the working of precious metals and stones has translated dreams and visions into highly creative works."

Alfredo Correnti has been creating handcrafted jewels since 1967. The transformation is the main theme in his artworks.

Angeletti 1940 is a historical Roman Maison, capable of harmonizing tradition and innovation. The Wave carpet bracelet is characterized by the deep contrast between the mother of pearl geometric golden profiled motifs and the chromatic combination of diamonds and carbon.

Cesari & Rinaldi Gemmai has been an important partner in the realization of custom-made gemstones for Fine and High Jewelry for more than forty years. The jewels displayed in this exhibition derive from the fruitful collaboration with the great artist Giò Pomodoro. The earrings, brooches and rings express Pomodoro's experimental style, his mastery in combining colors and gemstones and his continuous quest for innovation.

Giò Pomodoro wanted to create pieces that: "preserve the traditional values of the goldsmith art, the one-of-a-kind concept even in a mass production context".

Since 1943 de' Nobili has been creating jewelry enhancing each client's individual character. I Guerrieri bracelet (the warriors), made in collaboration with Sergio Fermariello, makes reference to powerful and archaic motifs.

Liverino 1894, a legend in the coral world,

has handed down over time this art at Torre del Greco. Over 1000 sculptural and jewelry pieces are displayed in the family museum. Rubrum Veritas (Red Truth) is a coral artistic skull in which Enzo Liverino experimented the double face theme with courage and passion.

The skull has not deliberately an ornamental or wearable function: yet it is a sculpture, a reflection about the meaning of life and an excellent experimentation.

Mattioli, refined ambassadors of Italian Jewelry, created the Harlequin puzzle earrings inspired by Joan Mirò's masterpiece "the Harlequin's Carnival", 1924.

Established in 1926, UNOAERRE is one of Italy's leading companies in the production, distribution and export of gold and jewelry. UNOAERRE and Giò Pomodoro partnership

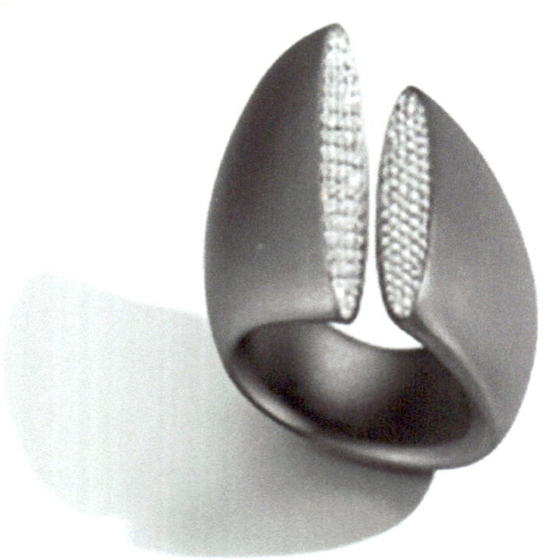

is one of the most fruitful collaborations in the history of the 20th century's art jewelry. Nuages is a bracelet designed by Giò Pomodoro in 1999. Vhernier, the famous Milanese Maison, has its own style fruit of research, accurate design and great quality of materials. Modern sculpture is the main source of inspiration: the result is bold, understated, elegant jewels that play with generous volumes and sensual lines. The rings on display at the exhibition are an emblem of Vhernier's style.

To conclude my article, I would like to thank the Club degli Orafi and Laura Biason for inviting me.

Laura Astrologo Porchè

la Meridiana

Albergo di charme in Garlenda dal 1978

★ ★ ★ ★ ★

**RELAIS &
CHATEAUX**

maya jah
MÉDITERRANÉEN & ORIENTAL

MAYA
ALTITUDE
RESTAURANT
MÉRIBEL

MAYA
MIA
RESTAURANT ITALIEN

REFUGE DE
la Traye
MÉRIBEL SAVOIE
Luxury Mountain Resort & Spa

MAYABAY
THAI - JAPANESE
MONACO

MAYA
Collection

ART

MONET'S HOUSE: A STEP INTO A WORK OF ART

About 50 minutes northwest of Paris lies the colorful village of Giverny, Normandy. This small town is home to the residence where Claude Monet lived and died. Entering Monet's house is like stepping through the gates of a small, independent state dedicated to art and nature. It is entering the heart of an artist's life. The entrance is through the most flowery garden in the world, always changing with the changing floral seasons. Designed by the artist to get lost in, letting your gaze wander among irises, nasturtiums, tulips, and rose bushes, gliding over the water lilies that, at the edge of the water, look like so many reflections. The world of the garden, in perpetual change depending on the seasons, dialogues with that of the house and the paintings on the walls. This country house, with its simple structure and all developed in length, had seduced the master of Impressionism. He discovered it by chance, walking through the fields, in love with the landscape and in search of motifs to paint. The encounter with Giverny took place in 1883, just in the middle of his life. It was love at first sight: for the place, for the surrounding spaces, and for the village.

In 1890, Monet bought the property and created his garden there. From the late 1890s, the themes of water, the water lily pond, waterscapes, and the garden marked about 40 years of the painter's creation.
"My most beautiful work of art is my garden." The garden, in fact, became the protagonist and symbol of everything that Monet depicted. He introduced three different elements: the reflection of the sky on the water, the depth of the pond in transparency, and the surface on which the water lilies float. From the first straight alleys to the

curved spaces of the streets surrounding the pond, from the promontory of the terrace in front of the house, to the panorama that extends from the Japanese bridge and the small walkway, Monet wanted to create a sequence of moving images.

The artist lived in this magical and unmissable place for the last 40 years of his life, with his second wife and their eight children. The rooms of the house are full of works by artists that Monet admired, such as Delacroix, Renoir, Cézanne, and Signac. On the ground floor, the most lived-in rooms are those covered with prints by great Japanese masters, of which he was an avid collector. Inside the house, visitors can meet the man in his daily life, between the blue tiled kitchen and the yellow dining room, without forgetting that that guest, as warm and welcoming as he was sometimes gloomy and tormented, was also, and above all, a master: the one who, with his Impressionist friends, revolutionized the history of art in the 19th century.

Anita Lodola

ARTE ARISTON
GALLERY

BEAUTY

ANGEL
Thierry Mugler
PARFUMS

ANGEL: AN ICON IN THE PERFUMERY SECTOR

Often in common memory the image of certain designers is associated with their creations that have become symbolic garments, just think of Cristobal Balenciaga's "Baby-Doll" dress or Dior's "Bar" suit in the 1950s. Leaping forward in time we land in the 1990s and meet Thierry Mugler, a revolutionary, innovative and multifaceted artist. Mentioning the Belgian designer one cannot but immediately think of one of the most iconic perfumes ever: Angel, still in the top 20 best-selling perfumes in the world. Mugler, driven and animated by the desire to create a perfume that was sweet, fun, unusual, and above all, never seen or heard of before, bequeathed us a true milestone in the world of fragrances: it is the most gourmand perfume ever, overflowing with symbols and hiding a myriad of secrets, and it revolutionized the perfumery industry.

It can be compared to a masterpiece, and as such it took years of work to find the perfect accord. At a time when unisex fragrances and floral bouquets dominated, the Belgian designer's perfume broke through with its sugary notes of vanilla, chocolate and caramel, expertly blended with fruity notes of bergamot, tangerine, peach and apricot, all offset by a mix of patchouli that lends an inimitable and unmistakable trail. The result was an intoxicating sweetness, also given by the artificial molecule of ethylmaltol, which gives caramelized nuances, but without being cloying and making Angel a transversal, feminine essence suitable for all women.

The years of research and refinement also served to devise a unique packaging: the five-pointed star was designed by Mugler himself, who had decided to create a casket that was conceived as a jewel, in the shape of a star precisely, because as he himself recounted, "In winter it gets dark very early in Alsace, I would find myself sitting on a bench in the little gardens watching the stars. They calmed me and reassured me, they were a magical and at the same time very real presence, far away, but also incredibly very close, sending me comforting signals, like angels." Through an exclusive, semi-crafted production process each star made is unique, but all stars are identical to each other. Angel also made its mark with its famous light blue, both in the packaging and in the fragrance itself, as if to further emphasize its connection to the world of magic and its ability to evoke pleasant thoughts and feelings.

Thanks to these characteristics, the fragrance designed by Mugler has to all intents and purposes taken on therole of an icon in the perfumery sector, never losing its importance and prestige even when special reinterpretations of it were presented (about a dozen), always addressing an extremely feminine, sweet and dreamy woman. Thus, from the desire to translate childhood memories into an engaging fragrance was born Angel, a celestial diamond forged in a five-pointed block of ice, capable of balancing decadence and pleasure, innocence and sensuality.

Chiara Collu

EVENTS

FRANCESCA RAVA FOUNDATION CHARITY GALA DINNER AND DANCE PARTY – NPH ITALIA ETS

Yacht Club of Monaco, 20 September 2023
A glamorous evening with Michelin-starred Chef Massimiliano Alajmo
Music by Alessandro Ristori and The Portofinos
Event for the benefit of the Foundation's environmental and social sustainability projects
The first Rava Foundation event in Monaco

The exclusive charity dance and gala dinner took place yesterday in the splendid setting of the Yacht Club of Monaco, organized by the Francesca Rava Foundation – NPH Italia ETS with the patronage of the Italian Embassy. Presence of Giulio Alaimo, Italian Ambassador in Monaco. The Francesca Rava Foundation presented more than twenty years of its work in favor of childhood and adolescence in Italy, Haiti and the world and presented the excellence of Italian cuisine and design during an evening dedicated to environmental and social sustainability, values that inspire all Foundation projects to achieve the Sustainable Development Goals of the United Nations 2030 Agenda (UNSDG).

An exclusive event attended by more than 350 friends and members of the Monegasque, French, Italian and international communities and many young volunteers, many of whom were high school students from Monaco who also enthusiastically participated in the volunteer camps of the Francesca Rava Foundation in Italy and in the NPH Foyers in Latin America. Martina Colombari, volunteer and ambassador of the Francesca Rava Foundation, participated in the event. On this occasion, prestigious companies such as CMB Monaco, KPMG, historical partner of the Foundation also for the balance sheet audit, and BANOR SIM SPA, which has always been close to the Foundation in major events and empowerment projects dedicated to young people, have chosen to support the Foundation. We are proud of the presence of Cristian Trio, entrepreneur in the real estate sector, founder of the Dyanema brand, specialized in real estate flipping operations and always at the forefront of humanitarian projects of the Francesca Rava Foundation. Vhernier has made available the reissue of the ring Pirouette «Vhernier for the children of Haiti». Each piece will contribute to the donation of a saving surgical operation for a hospitalized child at the NPH Saint Damien hospital, built and supported by the Foundation. Among the partners of the evening Le Due Vittorie, an Italian company of excellence producing balsamic vinegar. In addition, the excellence of the Italian design was represented by the installations of Armani Casa and by Kartell who took care of the installation and lighting and donated a unique piece for the auction, as well as by Alessi, Fornasetti, Roberta and Basta, who supported the evening by donating exclusive pieces from their collections. Brunello Cucinelli offered a unique experience to live in the charming village of Solomeo, thanks to a visit to the enchanting place and the cashmere company that has become, over time, a symbol of artisanal excellence. The city of Venice was the protagonist of the IFEXPERIENCE donation, which for the occasion offered an exclusive visit to some of the most fascinating sites of the lagoon city, usually closed to the public, accompanied by an expert in art history. The guests were welcomed at sunset with a welcome aperitif on the suggestive observation deck of the Yacht Club, made even more magical by the layout of Armani Casa, with a tasting of excellent Champagnes from Nero Lifestyle, including the Cuvée Croisade and the Rose De Damas, rare and precious French bubbles in limited edition to live a real sensory journey. The aperitif was accompanied by the music of Alessandro Martire, a renowned pianist who offers breathtaking performances in natural and urban contexts sought after worldwide. After the dinner placed in the Ballroom prepared by the Chef Massimiliano Alajmo, 3 Michelin stars, the youngest Chef in the world to obtain this prestigious recognition at only 28 years, also present with its restaurants in Sermerola di Rubano (PD) with Le Calandre, in Venice, Paris and the Royal Mansour in Marrakech. The

floral decoration of Marco Traverso & Histoires d'Ours made the atmosphere unique with its centerpieces, which the guests of the evening were able to take home with them thanks to a donation for children with disabilities hosted in the Maison des Petits Anges in Haiti. The dinner was accompanied by a fine selection of Masciarelli Tenute Agricole wines, including Villa Gemma Abruzzo Bianco DOC, with fruity and mineral notes, aromatic herbs and tropical fruits that give freshness and flavor. Gianni Masciarelli Cerasuolo d'Abruzzo DOC, obtained from 100% Montepulciano grapes from the vineyards of Loreto Aprutino, characterized by a bright cherry red color and intense scents and the Marina Cvetic Trebbiano d'Abruzzo DOC Riserva, an intense, rich and consistent wine, vinified and aged in barrels. Finally, the 2020 Vendanges Tardives – Château Imperial Tokaj, from the Gianni's Selection distribution line, was served with dessert. For the evening, Valverde donated little mineralized water that flows at the foot of Mount Rose, an uncontaminated UNESCO heritage area. La Pâtisserie Riviera delighted the guests with a fairy tale cake, offered to celebrate the arrival of the Francesca Rava Foundation in Monaco. The guests participated in the live dance performance of Alessandro Ristori and the Portofinos; a nationally and internationally renowned group, in the most important entertainment venues, with its irresistible rock of the 50s and 60s and professional dancers who animated the evening by training everyone in dance. The Hellenic Community of Monaco also joined the evening with President Sophia Vaharis Tsouvelekakis, who proposed special Greek cocktails based on ouzo and tsipouro at the time of the open bar. The event continued with a live auction, organized by Casa D'Aste Artcurial, with a selection of design objects, works of art and unique and exclusive experiences, such as the fabulous dinner at the Quadri di Venezia, the Doge's Ball in Venice and with a silent auction organized by Givergy, with many prizes, including some offered by the greatest sports champions, including Nadal, Musetti, Totti and Verratti, or by the largest Italian fashion houses. President Mariavittoria Rava: «The Francesca Rava Foundation has been involved in the organization of this evening with determination and love not only to bring concrete help to many children in serious difficulty in Haiti, Italy and the world, but also to convey the values of social and environmental sustainability that inspire all our projects». I would like to thank the Italian Embassy in Monaco and the institutions present at the event, the companies that with their excellence are at our side to share this unforgettable Gala, our wonderful young volunteers, donors, friends and all those who support us. To make lasting and concrete change in the lives of those who need it most, it is not enough to do good, but to do it in the best way possible: this is the philosophy of the Francesca Rava Foundation; for even good demands excellence. Join us and our work to save thousands of children in Italy, Haiti and around the world.

Jennifer Blaide

> Join us and our work to save thousands of children in Italy, Haiti and around the world

DYNAMIC

PIRELLI
P ZERO
PERONI
NASTRO AZZURRO
0.0%
cognizant
aramco
JCB
SentinelOne
ASTON MARTIN
cognizant
FORMULA ONE TEAM
cognizant
FERRARI

FERNANDO ALONSO THE COMEBACK

It was surprised and no-one saw it coming. The start of the 2023 Formula One World Championship has been nothing but phenomenal for the Aston Martin team, with star driver Fernando Alonso, on the back of two lacklustre seasons. In both 2021 and 2022, the Silverstone-based outfit finished seventh out of ten teams. After six races this year, Aston sits second in the constructors' table with Alonso a strong third in the drivers' championship, behind a dominant Red Bull team. It's even more remarkable considering the two-times world champion retired from F1 at the end of the 2018 season. Precisely, in 2018, after 17 seasons of dedicating his life to Formula1, Fernando Alonso had enough. With two world titles and 32 Grand Prix victories, he walked away. It had been 12 years since he was crowned champion and five since he had won a race. During Alonso short interview. When I finished, it was on a low, and didn't want that because my performance, my competitiveness, was as high as ever back then, but people didn't see it.

Now fast forward, he is proving still fast, at whatever age – thats part of the comeback story. Winning the 33rd Grand Prix or fighting for a championship would add even more drama to the story. After all, he was away from the sport for two years, 2019 and 2021 but during that time he continued to race and rediscovered the joy of winning. He became the world Endurance Champion with Toyota, took the checkered flag in the 24 Hours of Daytona and he won one of the most prestigious races in the world, the 24 Hours of "Le Mans" – not one but Twice.

One of the things that sets Alonso apart from other drivers is his ability to read a race. He has keen sense of what is happening on the track and can make split-second decisions that can make all the difference. He is clearly one of the greatest drivers to ever be in Formula 1 and his motivation has never been higher. However, despite his strong start of this season, it has been 10 years since Alonso 41, last won a Grand prix. Alonso returned to Formula 1 in 2021 with Alpine having moderate success, midway last summer caused a huge twist in F1's transfer by signing a deal with Aston Martin after only two seasons with Alpine. When I spoke to him, he said, "Listen, I can bring something to this team in my last few years I'm going to drive and hopefully have some sort of role within Aston Martin for many years to come after when I stop driving.

The agreement with Aston Martin was built on a friendship forged when Alonso first meet Lawrence Stroll (Aston Martin F1 Team Owner). Alonso said it made it easy for him and Stroll to turn their friendship into "A professional partnership". According to Stroll moving into the factory is imminent. The wind tunnel, which will allow the team to Aerodynamically test a scale model of a Formula 1 car, will open next Spring. With Alonso's performance,the results are ahead of forecast with the team in second place for constructors' title.

Fernando any thoughts about results?

I have been surprised by how quickly I have achieved results. I trusted the project and felt it was nice adventure for me at the end of my career, to start with a team that has so much enthusiasm and good aspects and I think 2024 we can fight for the podiums. I was not expecting the car would deliver the kind of performance we have now.

Second Retirement?

Definitely far from my thoughts, i am having too much fun again. I am aware of my age, I know I will not be here for the next 10 years,

or whatever, so maybe when I stop racing, I will be linked to the team somehow. I am hopeful that when that day comes again, my wait for win 33 will be over.

You're having tremendous success, What would you say about 33 Win?

Winning a championship would be a perfect thing, If I win another championship all these years since my previous one, that would be unprecedented, that kind of distance between two championships. That is my goal at the moment or the legacy that I want to leave in this sport, of someone who loves it so much that I kept racing for many years, keeping the level as high as possible. That would prove a point, something that was a part of my comeback.
In his 40's, Alonso's desire is massive and fitness are strong. The conditioning he has kept himself in physically and mentally and his motivation levels are higher than ever. He is absolutely determined to win.

Any Other Desire?

Although to win, ancther title are motivations but I have another desire. I want to have a family. This is my biggest dream in Life. I have still not succeeded in that because of my way of living. That's something that when I stop racing, where I will find my "Happiness".

Nancy Caburnay

ENJOY
EVEN MORE
FERNANDO
ALONSO

fondazione mente

MONACO
WOMAN

Editor & Founder	Alessia Castelli
Fashion Consultant	Piera Ghidotti Karine Patricola
Food & Hospitality Consultant	Nadia Toppino
Art Consultant	Anita Lodola
Motor Consultant	Nancy Caburnay
Travel Consultant	Claudia Rosso
Jewels Consultant	Laura Astrologo Porchè
Beauty Consultant	Chiara Collu
Book Consultant	Cristiana Girardi
Graphics & Layout	Jacopo Senni
Editor Assistant	Elena Andreetto
Photo Credits	Shutterstock, Mattia Aquila
Copyright	©2023. All rights reserved
Issue	00; Novembre 2023
ISBN	9798865234081
Periodicity	Two issues every year
Distribution	Amazon Kdp

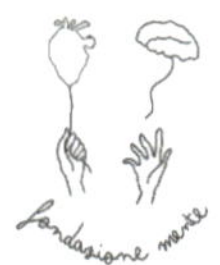

Ringrazio la mia famiglia, Massimo Basile, Krissy Pesciglione Cuni. Un ringraziamento particolare all'amico fraterno Marco Camisani Calzolari, che mi ha aiutata a trasformare questo sogno in realtà.